My Weird School
FAST FACTS

Pizza, Peanut Butter, and Pickles

My Weird School FAST FACTS

Pizza, Peanut Butter, and Pickles

Dan Gutman

Pictures by
Jim Paillot

HARPER

An Imprint of HarperCollinsPublishers

To Nina

The author gratefully acknowledges the editorial contributions of Nina Wallace. Photo credits: Page 9: Bozena Fulawka/Shutterstock; Page 12: Courtesy of the White House Collection/White House Historical Association; Page 16: LunaseeStudios/ Shutterstock; Page 17: foto76/Shutterstock; Page 22: Valentyn Volkov/Shutterstock; Page 29: Courtesy of the Library of Congress, LC-USZC4-599; Page 39: Csavvj; Page 45: LunaseeStudios/Shutterstock; Page 50: Bettmann/Getty Images; Page 56: M. Unal Ozmen/Shutterstock; Page 62: Courtesy of the Library of Congress, Chronicling America online collection; Page 72: Courtesy of Nationaal Archief; Page 82: US Department of Agriculture; Page 87: digitalreflections/Shutterstock; Page 91: Hulton Archive/Stringer/Getty Images; Page 97: Courtesy of the Missouri Historical Society, St. Louis, N16107; Page 110: Courtesy of the Library of Congress, LC-J601-302; Page 125: Collection of Auckland Museum Tāmaki Paenga Hira, 2015.4.50, Gift of Mrs. Yvonne Keesing; Page 130: Featureflash Photo Agency/Shutterstock; Page 144: tishomir/Shutterstock; Page 158: Handmade Pictures/Shutterstock; Page 162: abimages/Shutterstock; Page 173: Chicago History Museum/Contributor/Getty Images; Page 181: jesmo5/Shutterstock; Page 188: Leonard Zhukovsky/ Shutterstock; Page 194: darrenleejw/Shutterstock

ISBN 978-0-06-267315-2 (pbk. bdg.)–ISBN 978-0-06-267316-9 (library bdg.)

Typography by Laura Mock
19 20 21 22 23   PC/LSCH   10 9 8 7 6 5 4 3 2 1
❖
First Edition

Contents

Disclaimer: Nobody knows *for sure* who came up with the idea of putting stuff between two slices of bread and calling it a sandwich. Nobody knows *for sure* who the first person was to put sprinkles on an ice-cream cone. But over the years, many people have come to claim they were the first, or their grandmother was the first, or whatever. Some stories stand the test of time, and some don't. This book is filled with the stories that stood the test of time.

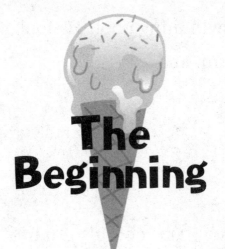

The Beginning

Howdy, weirdos! My name is Professor A.J., and I love food. I know lots of stuff about food that other kids don't know. Like, did you know that the ice-cream float was invented in 1912 when this guy named Bob was eating an ice-cream cone next to his swimming pool? He took one step backward, and—

 You're totally making that up, Arlo!

 Oh no! It's Andrea Young, that annoying girl in my class with curly brown hair! She calls me by my real name because she knows I don't like it. Who invited Little Miss I-Know-Everything?

 You know perfectly well that we're supposed to work on this project *together*, Arlo. And you don't have to make up silly stories about food.

The real facts are *so* interesting.

 It's true. Did you know that eating asparagus makes your pee smell?

 We're not going to discuss gross things here, Arlo! Remember we talked about that? No toilet stuff.

 Okay, okay! I'll save it for the end when you're not paying attention anymore. You're no fun at all.

 This is going to be *lots* of fun, Arlo! We're going to tell the

readers all kinds of cool stuff they don't know about food.

 I can tell them one thing right now. Food is weird.*

Sincerely,

Professor A.J.

(the professor of awesomeness)

 Andrea Young

(future Harvard graduate)

---

*I'm hungry already. What do we have to eat?

Chapter 1

Stuff That's Good for You

 Okay, let's start with candy, cake, cookies, chocolate, and other yummy foods that start with *C*.

 Arlo, *that* stuff isn't good for you. We should treat this project the same way we treat a meal. You eat the main course before you have dessert.

Let's start off by talking about the foods that are good for you. Like superfoods, for instance.

 Foods that give you super-powers? Cool!

 No! Superfoods are foods full of nutrients and antioxidants. They help prevent cancer, heart disease, and other diseases. Blueberries, spinach, kale, cabbage, broccoli, salmon, and sardines are superfoods.

 Ugh. I don't like *any* of that stuff!

 There are *lots* of foods that
are good for you, Arlo. Like
vegetables, for instance.

Nooooooooo! You said the *V* word! I'm not going to eat stuff that grows out of the dirt!

Weird Stuff about Veggies

 The first food grown in space was potatoes! Some potato plants were taken up in the space shuttle *Columbia* in 1995.

 Let's talk about tomatoes! For a long time, tomatoes were thought to be poisonous! People in Europe and the American colonies wouldn't eat them. The fear lasted until the late 1800s, and it ended in part thanks to the sudden popularity of a dish coming out of Naples: pizza with tomato sauce.

You probably think tomatoes are a vegetable, but technically they're a fruit. In 1893, the Supreme Court ruled that tomatoes could be taxed as veggies because they were used in regular meals. And they've been legally recognized as veggies since then.

Tomatoes are 94.5 percent water (and cucumbers are 95 percent water).

Let's talk about carrots! Did you ever hear that carrots help you see in the dark? Well, it's a myth. During World War II, the British didn't want the Germans to know about their advanced radar technology. So they spread the word that their pilots were successful in battle because they ate a lot of carrots! And people bought it!

Eating a lot of carrots can make your skin turn orange. Really! It's a medical condition called carotenemia. But don't worry. It's harmless.

There's a World Carrot Museum, and anybody can go there. It's online.

 Speaking of food museums,

there's a celery museum in Kalamazoo County, Michigan. By the way, in ancient Greece, the winners of athletic games were awarded a "bouquet of flowers"—made out of celery.

 I think I'd rather get a medal. Those Greeks were weird. Do you know what they used to treat toothaches? Asparagus!

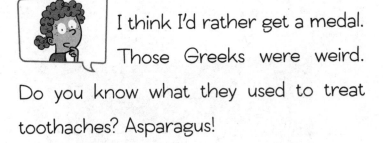 Asparagus really *does* makes your pee smell. You can look it up yourself. Or you can just eat a bunch of asparagus, drink a lot of water, and wait fifteen minutes.

President Thomas Jefferson loved broccoli, and he imported broccoli seeds from Italy to plant at his home. But President George H. W. Bush *hated* broccoli. It was a big story when he banned it from the White House.

President Thomas Jefferson

What's the number-one most hated veggie? There's one that always seems to top the list—Brussels sprouts. In a 2008 survey by the Heinz company, it was found to be the most hated vegetable in America. I bet they even hate it in Brussels!

Do you know the difference between red peppers and green peppers? There *is* no difference! Red peppers are just green peppers that have been left on the vine to ripen.

 You couldn't get a BLT sandwich in America until 1494. At least, that's when Christopher Columbus brought lettuce to the Americas. And it was another 400 years before somebody thought of adding bacon and tomato.

Speaking of lettuce, you should never store it with apples. They give off a gas called ethylene, which makes lettuce go bad much faster.

Do you know why onions make us cry?

 Because they tell really sad stories?

 No! It's because when you chop one up, it releases a chemical called lachrymatory factor that irritates the sensory nerves in our eyes.

 But do you know how to prevent yourself from crying while you're chopping up an onion? Hold a slice of bread in your mouth! You look ridiculous, but it works!

Popeye was a popular cartoon character who was famous for loving spinach. Whenever Popeye had to fight a bad guy, he would eat a can of spinach. Suddenly, his muscles would get big and he'd start beating the bad guy up. During the 1930s, spinach sales zoomed because of Popeye.

Weird Stuff about Fruit

 Fruit is good for you too, Arlo. Let's talk about fruit.

 Okay. The durian is an Asian fruit that smells like rotting meat. It stinks so bad that it's banned from the Singapore train system.

Ever hear of Granny Smith apples? They were named after Maria Ann Sherwood Smith, an Australian woman who found them growing in her orchard in the 1860s.

 The Jamaican tangelo is a combination of grapefruit, orange, and tangerine. It's also called Ugli fruit. Do you want to know why?

 Because it's ugly?

 Yes! Let's talk about bananas! If you ask me, bananas are

the funniest fruit. They have a funny shape. They're spelled funny. And it sounds funny to say banana!

Bananas are picked and shipped when they're green, because the ripe yellow ones are too delicate. It you want to ripen a banana fast, put it in a bag with an apple or a tomato.

Most of the bananas we eat are Cavendish bananas, and every single one is genetically the same. So a single fungus or disease could kill them all. It happened once before. Up until the 1950s, the most popular banana in the world was called the Gros Michel. That's when a disease wiped almost all of them out.

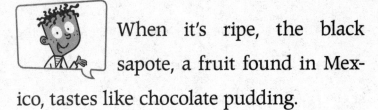 When it's ripe, the black sapote, a fruit found in Mexico, tastes like chocolate pudding.

The orange Yubari King melon is the world's most expensive fruit. In 2016, two of them sold at auction in Japan for $27,000.

 Do you know what is the most popular fruit in the world?

 Froot Loops?

 Froot Loops don't even have fruit in them! The fruit that's

eaten in more countries than any other is mango.

 That was my next guess. When you buy an apple at the market, it could have been picked a year ago. Apples can be put in "controlled atmosphere storage," so they sort of go to sleep until they're shipped to the markets.

Oranges have a lot of vitamin C. But did you know that a kiwi half the size of an orange has just as much vitamin C? One kiwi is 100 percent of your recommended daily value.

Japanese farmers sometimes grow

melons inside glass boxes so they grow in the shape of a cube. That makes them easier to stack and store, but it also makes them nearly inedible, because they have to be harvested before they're ripe.

 When is an orange not orange? When it's yellow or green! In Brazil, where they grow more oranges than any other country, oranges are sometimes different colors because of the high temperatures there.

Cherry farmers rent helicopters to fly over their trees after a rain. This air dries the trees so that the cherries don't split open.

Back in the 1840s, John "Peg Leg" Webb dropped a batch of cranberries down the stairs and discovered that they bounced! And the higher they bounce, the better the berry! In

fact, today cranberry farmers sort cranberries with a "bounce board separator."

Apple trees grow apples, of course.
Pear trees grow pears. But did you know

there are fruit salad trees that grow as many as six different kinds of fruit on the same tree?

 Pineapples were very expensive in colonial times. American colonists wanted to make people think they were wealthy, so they'd rent a pineapple and carry it around at parties. That's just pathetic.

Weird Stuff about Beans and Nuts

 Beans and nuts are good for you too. They have lots of protein. Arlo, do you know what legumes are?

Sure. That's gum you put on your legs.

 No, dumbhead! Legumes are peas and beans. In ancient Rome, four leading families took their names from legumes: Lentullus (lentil), Piso (pea), Cicero (chickpea), and Fabius (fava).

 The Romans were weird. But the ancient Greeks were even weirder. They would elect some politicians by putting a white bean with a bunch of black beans in a "bean machine." Whoever picked the white bean won the election. The ancient Greeks also thought hazelnuts could cure baldness.

 Let's talk about beans. Did you know that over 71,000 people in the world have the last name Bean?

 Of course. Did you know that people in Vermont search for bean recipes online more than people in any other state?

 Everybody knows that. Did you know that newlyweds in Nicaragua are given a bowl of beans for good luck?

Sure. But here's the ultimate bean fact. Are you sitting down? In 1986, Barry "Captain Beany" Kirk from England sat in a bathtub full of cold baked beans for a hundred hours. That's just nuts.

 Let's talk about nuts. Two peanut farmers became president of the United States—Thomas Jefferson and Jimmy Carter.

President Jimmy Carter

Mr. Klutz is nuts. Did you know that macadamia nuts are toxic to dogs?

 I did. Did you know it takes about 540 peanuts to make a jar of peanut butter? And did you know why peanuts are called goobers? In the Congo, the word for peanuts is *nguba*.

 I know all that stuff. Did you know that six towns in the United States are named Peanut? There are Peanuts in California, Tennessee, and West Virginia, and *three* Peanuts in

Pennsylvania—Upper Peanut, Lower Peanut, and—

 Let me guess. Peanut! But did you know that peanuts aren't even nuts—technically, they're legumes.

 Not with the legumes again! Okay, here's the nuttiest nut fact of all. In 1971, Alan Shepard, an astronaut on *Apollo 14*, brought a peanut with him to the moon.

 Why?

 Nobody knows. He also brought a golf club with him. That was weird.

 Ms. Beard is weird.

Chapter 2

Stuff That's Not So Good for You

 Okay, now that we've covered the foods that are good for you, I guess it's time to talk about the foods that aren't so good for you.

 Yay! The *good* stuff! It's about time! I love cookies and junk food. Candy was the greatest invention in the history of the world. If we didn't have candy—

 Calm down, A.J. Do you even know why candy and junk food taste so good?

 Who cares? As long as I can eat it.

 It's all because of sugar. Sugar is a carbohydrate called sucrose, and it can come from sugarcane or the root of the sugar beet plant. Maple syrup and honey are also made of sugar. And some foods—like fruits, vegetables, and dairy products—contain natural sugars.

Sugar doesn't have any essential nutrients in it. No protein, no vitamins, and no minerals. It can cause tooth decay and obesity. That doesn't mean we should never eat sugar. But we should be careful not to eat too much of it.

 Zzzzzzzz . . . Oh, sorry, I dozed off there for a few minutes. We were about to talk about candy, right?

A Handy Candy Timeline

 In school, we learn about the

history of wars, inventions, famous people, and all that other boring stuff. Why don't they teach kids the history of cool stuff? Like candy!

Well, today is your lucky day. Arlo and I put together this handy candy timeline. We didn't have room to include *every* kind of candy. But a lot of your favorites are here. . . .

1845: Young & Smylie Company in Brooklyn, New York, begins making licorice candies. It became the National Licorice Company in 1902, and in 1929 it introduced Twizzlers.

1847: A Boston pharmacist named

Oliver Chase invents a machine for cutting candy into pieces.

 1848: John Curtis makes the first commercial chewing gum from tree sap he cooked in his wife's pots. It was called State of Maine Pure Spruce Gum.

1868: Richard and George Cadbury, two brothers in England, make the first Valentine's Day box of chocolates.

 1875: Swiss chocolate maker Daniel Peter adds condensed milk to chocolate and invents . . . milk chocolate!

1880s: George Renninger of Philadelphia invents candy corn. It didn't get popular until ten years later, when it was sold under the name Chicken Feed.

1888: Tutti-Frutti chewing gum becomes the first gum sold from a vending machine.

1893: Good & Plenty is introduced by Quaker City Confectionery Company of Philadelphia. It's the oldest brand name candy still in production. The same year, William Wrigley Jr. of Chicago introduces Juicy Fruit and Wrigley's Spearmint Chewing Gum.

1896: Leo Hirschfield introduces Tootsie Rolls. He named them after his daughter's nickname, Tootsie.

1897: Cotton candy is invented by Nashville dentist (!) William Morrison and candy maker John C. Wharton. At first, they called it fairy floss.

 1900: Milton Hershey introduces Hershey's Milk Chocolate Bar.

1901: Necco Wafers are born. The name stands for New England Confectionery Company.

 1906: Chiclets, the first candy-coated gum, is introduced.

1907: Hershey's Kisses are introduced. They were once called Silvertops.

1911: Mars, Inc. is started by Ethel and Frank Mars in Tacoma, Washington.

1912: Life Savers are invented by Clarence Crane of Cleveland, Ohio. They got their name because they looked like little life preservers.

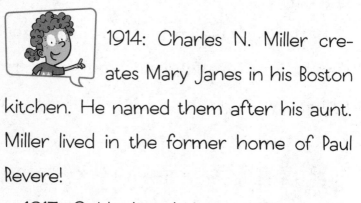 1914: Charles N. Miller creates Mary Janes in his Boston kitchen. He named them after his aunt. Miller lived in the former home of Paul Revere!

1917: Goldenberg's Peanut Chews are created for American troops in World War I.

1920: Williamson Candy Company in Chicago introduces the Oh Henry! bar. The same year, Henry Heidi, a German immigrant, invents Jujyfruits and Jujubes. Also, in Bonn, Germany, Hans Riegel invents gummy bears in his home kitchen.

1921: A big year for candy. Fred W. Amend owns a marshmallow factory in Danville, Illinois. That's where he invents a colorful jelly candy, which he names Chuckles. The same year, the Mounds bar is invented by an Armenian immigrant named Peter Paul Halajian in New Haven, Connecticut.

Finally, the Curtiss Candy Company of Chicago introduces the Baby Ruth bar, which some say was named after the baseball player Babe Ruth, and others say was named after President Grover Cleveland's daughter.

1923: Mars introduces the Milky Way bar. It wasn't named after our galaxy. It was named after a famous malted milk drink of the time.

1924: Dum Dums lollipops are introduced by the Akron Candy Company in Bellevue, Ohio. Their sales manager suggested the name. He said "dum dums" were words any toddler could say.

1926: Milk Duds are introduced by F. Hoffman &
Company of Chicago. They wanted to
make round chocolate-covered caramels,
but there was a problem with the machin-
ery. A worker said they were "duds," and
the company decided to go with that
name.

1928: Harry Burnett Reese leaves Hershey to start his own candy company. He

combines peanut butter with Hershey's milk chocolate, and Reese's Peanut Butter Cups are born. The same year, bubble gum is invented! The Fleer Chewing Gum Company in Philadelphia introduces Dubble Bubble.

 1930: Snickers are introduced. They were named after a racehorse owned by the Mars family.

1931: If one kind of candy is good, two is even better! Tootsie Pops are introduced.

 1932: Mars is on a roll. They introduce 3 Musketeers. At first, it was three little bars with chocolate, vanilla, and strawberry nougat inside. When sugar was rationed during World War II, they switched to just the one bar with chocolate nougat that we know today.

1941: M&M's are introduced, also from Mars. The two *M*'s stand for Forrest Mars and Bruce Murrie, who was the son of Hershey president William Murrie.

1947: Bazooka bubble gum is introduced by Topps Candy Company of Brooklyn, New York. It was named after a 1930s musical instrument with two gas pipes and a funnel. It wasn't until 1953 that each piece was wrapped with a Bazooka Joe comic.

1949: Smarties is introduced by Ce De Candy Company in Bloomfield, New Jersey. Inventor Edward Dee was a Cambridge University graduate, and he named the candy Smarties to encourage education.

1951: Topps adds free baseball cards to their bubble gum packages. Now it can cost more than two million dollars for a 1952 Topps Mickey Mantle rookie card.

1954: Just Born Candy Company in Bethlehem, Pennsylvania, introduces Marshmallow Peeps in the shape of Easter chicks.

1967: Starburst arrives in America. They were invented in England with the name Opal Fruits.

1975: Pop Rocks are introduced! They are cool. As they melt in your mouth, tiny air pockets of carbonation (CO_2) are released and you feel a crackling, fizzing sensation. A rumor started that if you mixed Pop Rocks with soda, your stomach would explode!

1976: Jelly Belly arrives. They're individually flavored jelly beans. A few years later, they become popular because President Ronald Reagan was a fan.

Bob Dole and Ronald Reagan with a jar of jelly beans at a meeting in Washington, 1984

1978: Reese's Pieces are introduced. They take off in 1982 when they're featured in the movie *E.T. the Extra-Terrestrial.*

 1979: Frank Richards's baby daughter sucks her thumb all the time, so he invents something to help her kick the habit—the Ring Pop!

1980: Two professional baseball players—Rob Nelson and Jim Bouton—create Big League Chew. It's shredded bubble gum in a pouch.

 1985: Sour Patch Kids come to America. For years, they were available in Canada under the name Mars Men.

I Scream, You Scream . . .

If you read *Mr. Will Needs to Chill!*, you know how much I love ice cream. It's my favorite food, except for chocolate, cupcakes, candy,

and cookies. I'll eat anything that starts
with a *C.*

 How about cockroaches?

 Uh, except that.

 Do you know who invented
ice cream?

 Bob Ice Cream?

 Arlo, everybody who invented

anything was *not* named Bob. The truth is, *nobody* knows who invented ice cream. In China around 200 BCE, people ate a milk and rice mixture that was frozen by packing it into snow. Alexander the Great liked to eat snow and ice that was flavored with honey and nectar. Roman emperors used to send runners into the mountains to get snow, and then it was flavored with fruits and juices.

 Marco Polo came back to Italy from the Far East with a recipe that was a lot like our sherbet. Ice cream appeared in England in the 1600s, except they called it cream ice. Maybe they ate it backward.

 Back then, ice cream was just for rich people. But in 1686, regular people could get it for the first time. Café Le Procope in Paris became famous for its ice cream desserts.

 America's founding fathers enjoyed ice cream too. George Washington spent two hundred dollars for ice cream during the summer of 1790. I wonder if his sweet tooth was made out of wood.

 Do you know how the ice-cream sundae was invented?

 Of course. This guy named Bob Sunday didn't know how to spell his own name—

 No! During the late nineteenth century, it was illegal to sell ice-cream sodas on Sunday in Evanston, Illinois.

 How come?

 Soda was considered to be a dangerous medicine back then, so people felt it had to be regulated, like alcohol. To get around the problem, vendors replaced the soda with syrup and called the ice cream treat an ice cream Sunday. When church leaders complained that Sunday was a holy day, the spelling was changed to sundae.

 The five most popular ice-cream flavors, according to the International Dairy Foods Association, are vanilla, chocolate, cookies and cream, mint chocolate chip, and chocolate chip cookie dough.

Cola Wars

Soda is the coolest drink because it makes you burp. Soda is "carbonated," which means those little bubbles in it have carbon dioxide in them. As you drink it, that gas collects in your stomach. After a while, your digestive system wants to get rid of the carbon dioxide, so you burp. Want to hear me burp the alphabet?

 No.

 How about "Yankee Doodle"?

 No. Burping is disgusting.

 Okay. Want to talk about some of our favorite drinks?

 Sure.

Dr Pepper

 Dr Pepper is the oldest soda that we still drink today. It was invented in 1885 by a pharmacist named Charles Alderton in Waco, Texas. In fact, Dr Pepper, Coca-Cola, and Pepsi were *all* invented by pharmacists. Ever since Roman times, natural mineral water was thought to have healing powers. Alderton sold Dr Pepper as an energy drink and "brain tonic."

Why is it called Dr Pepper? One theory is that it was named after Dr. Charles T. Pepper, a Virginia pharmacist.

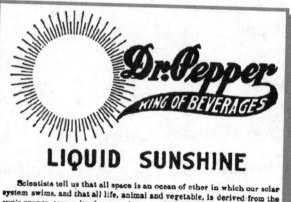

LIQUID SUNSHINE

Scientists tell us that all space is an ocean of ether in which our solar system swims, and that all life, animal and vegetable, is derived from the sun's energy, transmitted to our planet by this ether. Plant life organizes this energy for us in natures laboratory. As animals we then partake of natures bountiful store and the sun's energy. Certain fruits, nuts and sugar cane represent this energy and vitality best. We have found this great natural law, and we combine these substances with distilled water. The name we give our combination is Dr. Pepper.

Dr. Pepper is liquid sunlight. As the sun rules and governs the day, so should you govern your appetite. Eat and drink to build up the cells that are broken down by fatigue, mental or physical. Drink a beverage that promotes cell building, not one that simply deadens the sensory nerves. Drink Dr. Pepper. Solar energy-liquid sunshine. Vim, vigor, vitality—that is what Dr. Pepper means. Try it. On sale at all fountains and in bottles. It's made in Texas. It's profits are spent in Texas to promote Texas industries,

DR. PEPPER CO. Waco, Texas

Coca-Cola

 A year after Dr Pepper was invented, pharmacist John S.

Pemberton in Atlanta, Georgia, invented Coke. He wanted to make a tasty syrup that could be sold at soda fountains, where it would be mixed with carbonated water. Pemberton combined water with kola nut extract, caffeine, wine, and coca leaves. He called  the drink Pemberton's French Wine Coca. Later the wine was removed and replaced with sugar syrup. The result was called Coca-Cola, or more often, just Coke.

Pepsi-Cola

 In 1893, a pharmacist named Caleb Bradham invented Pepsi-Cola in New Bern, North Carolina. He called it Brad's Drink at first and changed it to Pepsi-Cola in 1898. Why? Because "dyspepsia" means indigestion, and Pepsi was supposed to calm the stomach.

Pepsi and Coke taste very similar, and many people can't tell them apart in blind taste tests. For the last hundred years or so, Coca-Cola and Pepsi-Cola have been fighting what was called in the advertising world a cola war.

7UP

 Charles Leiper was not a pharmacist. He was an advertising man in St. Louis, Missouri. But he was also a part-time inventor. He invented a soda called Whistle and another one called Howdy. But he didn't hit it big until 1929, when he invented a drink called Bib-Label Lithiated Lemon-Lime Soda. Terrible name, right? In 1936, the name was changed to 7UP.

Why 7UP? There are theories: It had seven ingredients. There are seven letters in "Seven Up." It was sold in seven-ounce bottles. The real answer: nobody knows.

Mountain Dew

 Another lemon-lime soda was invented by two brothers from Knoxville, Tennessee—Barney and Ally Hartman—in 1932. The original mascot of the drink was Willy the Hillbilly, who said, "It'll tickle yore innards."

Gatorade

 In 1965, the coach of the Florida Gators football team asked the University of Florida to come up with a drink that would help his players replace the bodily fluids they lost during games. Dr. Robert Cade and his team came up with Gatorade. Two years later, the Gators won their first Orange Bowl. When the opposing coach was asked why they lost, he said, "We didn't have Gatorade. That made the difference."

The History of Chocolate

 We had to save the best for last. Chocolate is the greatest food in the history of the world. We should eat it at every meal, and between meals too. And between between meals. We should just eat it all the time.*

---

*But not when we're sleeping or taking a shower. That would be weird.

People have been eating chocolate for thousands of years. Montezuma, who was the emperor of the ancient Aztec civilization, enjoyed a drink with cocoa beans called *chocolatl*. So did the ancient Mayans. In fact, both the Mayans and Aztecs used cocoa beans as if they were money. The beans were thought to be worth more than gold dust.

 Columbus brought cocoa beans back to Spain in 1504 and gave them to King Ferdinand and Queen Isabella as a treasure from the Americas. That's how chocolate came to Europe.

Napoléon, the French emperor, loved chocolate. He insisted that it be given to him during battles.

 Back in those days, chocolate was just a drink. During the Industrial Revolution, people started inventing machines that changed the way people ate chocolate. A Frenchman named Doret made a machine to grind cocoa beans into paste. Another Frenchman named Dubuisson invented a steam-driven machine that could grind large amounts of cocoa. Chocolate could now be mass-produced quickly and

cheaply so people who weren't wealthy could buy it.

 In 1829, a Dutch chemist named Coenraad Van Houten invented a machine that squeezed the cocoa butter out of the bean, leaving the powder we call cocoa. He also added alkaline salts to powdered chocolate to help it mix better with water and make it smoother, creamier, and tastier. The whole process is called dutching in honor of Van Houten.

 Finally, in 1847, Joseph Fry from England created the

Coenraad Van Houten

formula to mix cocoa powder, sugar, and cocoa into a paste that could then be pressed into a mold. The chocolate bar was born! Joseph Fry is the greatest man in the history of the world.

Weird Facts about Chocolate . . .

 Most of the world's cocoa—70 percent—comes from West Africa. The country that produces the most—the Ivory Coast.

 White chocolate is *not* chocolate. It's made by combining cocoa butter with sugar, milk solids, and vanilla flavoring.

 For the 1971 movie *Willy Wonka and the Chocolate Factory,* the crew made a chocolate river with fifteen thousand gallons of water mixed

with chocolate and cream. During the filming, the river "went bad" and smelled horrible for days.

 M&M's used to have the slogan "Melts in your mouth, not in your hand." Chocolate is the only edible substance that melts at 93°F, which is below our average body temperature. That's why it melts in your mouth.

 According to *Guinness World Records*, the biggest chocolate bar ever was created in England. It weighed 12,770 pounds.

 Did you ever hear that you should never give chocolate to dogs? In fact, it can kill them! Chocolate has this stuff called theobromine in it.

Our bodies can process theobromine easily, but dogs can't.

 In 2013, the post office in Belgium issued chocolate-flavored stamps.

 You'll like this, Arlo. Chocolate has an enzyme called phenyl-ethylamine. When you eat a piece of chocolate, it releases hormones in your brain that give you a feeling like being in love.

 Ugh! Gross! You said the *L* word! I'll never eat chocolate again!

There are bugs in candy bars. It's true! In fact, most foods we eat have tiny amounts of natural contaminants in them. The average chocolate bar contains eight insect parts. If there are more than sixty insect pieces per one hundred grams, the chocolate is rejected by the US Food and Drug Administration.

 That's it! I'm not eating bugs. I've had it. No more chocolate for me, ever.

So What Should We Eat?

 Arlo, did you know that even

food that's good for you can kill you?

 Well, sure. If a truck full of watermelons fell on your head—

 No, I mean *eating* some foods can kill you. The stalks of the rhubarb plant are fine to eat, but the leaves contain this really dangerous stuff called oxalic acid. It's a chemical found in bleach, metal cleaners, and anti-rust products. And if you take certain medications, eating grapefruit can kill you. And you should never eat the pit of an apricot, because it contains cyanide. Oh, and the shell of the cashew nut is toxic. Cashews are in the same plant family as poison ivy and poison sumac. And then there's fugu, the poisonous pufferfish that will kill you . . .

 Wait. Now let me get this straight. Junk food is bad for me.

 Right.

 And good foods can kill me.

 Under certain circumstances, yes.

 So what *should* I eat?

 I'm glad you asked, Arlo. Did you ever hear of MyPlate? It's a nutritional guideline created by the US Department of Agriculture (USDA). It breaks up our diet into five food groups: vegetables, fruits, grains, proteins, and dairy. You can see that fruits and veggies take up half the plate. Grains and protein take up the other half. And there's a small amount of dairy on the side. The right combinations of food will help you be healthy and keep you healthy as you grow up.

ChooseMyPlate.gov

 Can't I just fill up the whole plate with junk food?

 You could, but that wouldn't

be very good for you. You should save junk food as a treat for special occasions.

 You forgot one thing, Andrea.

 What?

 Water! We should drink lots of it. Drinking water helps maintain the balance of our body fluids. It helps energize our muscles.

 That's right! Our bodies are composed of about 60

percent water. Without water, our bodies would stop working properly.

 Drinking water also helps us poop.

 Somehow I knew you were going to find a way to get pooping into this book.

Chapter 3

Oops! Foods Invented by Mistake

Chocolate Chip Cookies

 Ruth Wakefield and her husband ran the Toll House Inn in Whitman, Massachusetts, and Ruth prepared all the food. One night in the 1930s, she decided to make chocolate cookies for the guests. The only problem was that she was out of baker's chocolate. So she chopped up a block of Nestlé semisweet chocolate she had lying around. She thought it would melt like regular baking chocolate. But it didn't. The chocolate pieces were scattered all over the cookie, and the chocolate chip cookie was born.

Word got around, and sales of Nestlé semisweet chocolate went through the roof. Nestlé offered Ruth a lifetime supply of free chocolate, and they started selling pre-chopped chocolate chips called Nestlé Toll House Real Semi-Sweet Chocolate Morsels. Ruth Wakefield's recipe was on the package, and it's still there today.

Sadly, the Toll House Inn caught on fire and burned down in 1984. A sign there marks where the chocolate chip cookie was born.

Nachos

 Ignacio Anaya worked at a restaurant called the Victory

Club in Mexico. One day in 1943, a group of ladies came in to eat. For some reason, the chef wasn't around. Ignacio didn't know what to say. He didn't know what to do. He had to think fast! So he covered a plate of tostadas with grated cheese and put it in the broiler to melt the cheese. Then he put some jalapeños on top. The ladies loved the new dish. Because Ignacio's nickname was "Nacho," he called it Nacho's *especiale* (Nacho's "special"). And the rest is snacking history.

 By the way, the microwave oven was also invented by accident. In 1945, an engineer named

Percy Spencer was working on radar for a company called Raytheon. He was experimenting with microwaves when he noticed that a candy bar in his pocket had melted. And the rest is history.

The Sandwich

 Do you know who invented the sandwich, Arlo?

 Bob Sandwich?

 It was John Montagu, Fourth Earl of Sandwich in England.

There are a few theories about how it happened. One says Montagu was in an intense gambling game in 1762 and didn't want to leave the game for a meal. So he ordered his cook to prepare him something he could eat without leaving the table. The cook brought to him some beef between two pieces of bread. Another theory says Montagu was working at his desk for many hours, so he needed a meal he could eat without having to use a knife and fork. Nobody knows which theory is right. But we can thank the Earl of Sandwich for this great invention.*

---

*And we can thank my friend Ryan for the invention of the wichsand. That's a sandwich with the meat on the outside and the bread in the middle.

The Right Honble The EARL of SANDWICH

Potato Chips

Legend has it that one day in 1853, a chef named George Crum was working at a restaurant in Saratoga Springs, New York. A customer ordered fried potatoes, and George cooked them up. But the customer sent them back, complaining that they weren't thin enough.

George was a little annoyed, but you know what they say—the customer is always right. So George fried up a new batch of fried potatoes that were sliced thinner.

The customer sent them back again.

Well, by that time, George was getting angry. So he sliced up some potatoes ridiculously thin. He salted them, fried them, and had them delivered to the annoying customer. That'll show him!

As it turned out, the customer *loved* the thinly sliced fried potatoes! Word got around about how good they were, and they came to be known as the "Saratoga Chip."

Cheese Puffs and Pop-Tarts

 Cheese puffs were invented by a company that made food for cows! In 1935, Edward Wilson was working for Flakall Company in Beloit, Wisconsin. The company made feed for livestock, using a grinding machine that turned kernels of corn into flakes. To prevent the machine from clogging, the workers would pour moist corn into it. Airy puffs of corn would shoot out, and they hardened when they hit the air.

Wilson decided to take some puffs home to experiment with, and he added oil, cheese, and seasonings. The result was . . . delicious! He called the new food Korn Kurls. They were so popular that Flakall Company ended up changing its name to Adams Corporation, at least partly so people wouldn't think their snacks were intended for cows.

 Pop-Tarts also came from the animal world. In 1961, Post developed a dog food called Gaines Burgers that was moist but didn't have to be refrigerated. They decided to try the same idea with food for people in the form of fruit filling that would stay moist and safe to eat without needing to be refrigerated, creating a pastry called Country Squares.

Before they were available in stores, Kellogg's introduced their own fruit-flavored Pop-Tarts. The name was a play on the pop art movement of the 1960s.

Ice-Cream Cone

 It's so simple. You take some ice cream and put it in a cone to eat it. No dishes or spoon to wash. They've probably been doing that for a thousand years, right? Well, the truth is that before 1904, nobody in the world had ever eaten an ice cream cone.

At the World's Fair in St. Louis that year, an ice cream vendor sold so much

WORLD'S FAIR, ST. LOUIS. 1904.

ice cream that he ran out of dishes. The guy in the booth next to him was Ernest Hamwi, an immigrant from Syria. He was selling a thin, crispy pastry called *zalabia*. When the ice cream vendor ran out of dishes, Hamwi offered him some *zalabia* to put the ice cream in. I don't need to tell you what happened after that.

By the way, another immigrant invented the cone

itself. Italo Marchiony came from Italy to sell lemon ices on the streets of New York. In his spare time, he invented a machine to roll cones. Legend has it that Marchiony was at the St. Louis World's Fair, and he was the ice cream vendor who ran out of dishes. But legends are legends, of course.

Slurpees

 When he came home after World War II, Omar Knedlik bought a Dairy Queen in Kansas. The soda fountain was constantly breaking down, so one day in 1958, Omar put some soda pop in a freezer to keep it cool. Then he forgot about it. When he served half-frozen sodas to his customers, they said they actually liked it that way.

A friend suggested the name ICEE for the slushy soda, and Omar advertised it as "the coldest drink in town." There was so much demand that Omar built a new machine to make ICEEs, and he started selling *them* too. In 1965, 7-Eleven licensed the machine and renamed the drink Slurpee.

Corn Flakes

 When you pick an ear of corn,

you don't see *flakes*. You see kernels. Somebody had to *turn* those kernels into flakes. Those somebodies were Will Kellogg and Dr. John Kellogg. The brothers ran a sanitarium in Battle Creek, Michigan, and they were always trying to come up with healthy foods that their patients would like.

One day in 1898, they accidentally let some boiled wheat go stale. Instead of throwing away the batch, they tried rolling it. It cracked into flakes. Hmmm, interesting! Then the Kellogg brothers toasted the flakes and asked their patients to taste them. They liked the toasted flakes so much that Will and John experimented with other grains. Corn was a natural. And breakfast was never the same.

We'll talk more about the Kellogg brothers in chapter five.

Chapter 4

Halftime!

 Well, we've reached the middle of the book, Arlo. And you know what that means.

 It's halftime?

 Yes! So it's time for some halftime entertainment. Do you know any food jokes?

Sure I do. What do you call cheese that isn't yours?

Nacho cheese. Get it? Not your cheese?

 I get it. Why did the fisher-man drop peanut butter into the ocean?

To go with the jellyfish.

 What's green and sings?

Elvis Parsley.

What did the baby corn say to its mom?

"Where is pop corn?"

 Why should you never tell a secret on a farm?

Because the potatoes have eyes and the corn has ears.

 Why did the teddy bear say no to dessert?

Because he was stuffed.

 Why did the baker stop making doughnuts?

He was tired of the hole business.

 What did the skeleton order for dinner?

Spare ribs.

 Why did the tomato turn red? Because it saw the salad dressing.

 What should you give to a sick lemon?

Lemonade. Get it? Lemon aid?

 I get it. What starts with *T*, ends with *T*, and is filled with *T*?

A teapot.

Why should you stare at the carton of orange juice?

Because it says "concentrate" on it.

 Why did the bear eat the tightrope walker?

He wanted a balanced meal.

What's the difference between a grape and a chicken?

They're both purple, except for the chicken.

 What did the gingerbread man put on his bed?

A cookie sheet.

 What did the oil and vinegar say to the refrigerator?

"Close the door, we're dressing."

Chapter 5

Famous Foodies

Do you know who invented the spatula? It was Bob Spatula of Oak Park, Illinois. One day, he was making pancakes in his kitchen when a big glop of pancake batter—

Arlo, that is a total lie! There's no such person as Bob Spatula!

I know. I was just yanking your chain. But here are some *real* food pioneers who changed the world . . .

George Washington Carver (1864–1943)

 Born a slave in Missouri, George Washington Carver went on to become a famous inventor, chemist, botanist, and scientist.

Carver was famous for his work with peanuts. Yes, peanuts! He found hundreds of ways to use them, and not just as food products. He turned peanuts into dyes for clothing, fuel for cars, insulation, and even soap. The guy was just nutty about peanuts!

Luther Burbank (1849–1926)

 What do you get when you cross a plum with an apricot? A plumcot! That was just one creation of botanist, horticulturist, and scientist Luther Burbank. He was called the "Plant Magician" because he seemed to do magic using plants. It was Burbank who invented the Elberta peach, the Shasta daisy, the California wildflower, and over eight hundred other plants, fruits, flowers, and vegetables.

Burbank's most famous creation was the "Russet Burbank potato," the most common potato used today. McDonald's uses it for their French fries.

Clarence Birdseye (1886–1956)

 Does your family cook frozen

pizza? How about frozen TV dinners? Frozen peas or corn? If the answer is yes, you owe a big thank-you to Clarence Birdseye. He invented frozen food.

In 1912, Birdseye took a trip to Canada, where he went ice fishing. Birdseye noticed that when a fish was caught and it was really cold outside—like -40°F—the fish froze almost instantly. He also noticed that when it was later thawed out and cooked, it tasted *great*!

Birdseye experimented with "flash freezing" other foods, and created a company to sell them. If you go into the frozen food aisle of any supermarket, you'll see lots of stuff made by the Birds Eye company.

Louis Pasteur (1822–1895)

 Go get a carton of milk. Look at the carton. It says the milk is pasteurized. But what does that mean? It means that before the milk got to the store, it was heated to a high temperature for a short period of time. That killed harmful bacteria, so the milk would last longer and be safe for you to drink.

That process was invented by a Frenchman named Louis Pasteur in 1862. It was so effective that it was named after him.

Today, pasteurization is used not just for milk but also for fruit juice, eggs, cheese, wine, and beer.

Milton Hershey (1857–1945)

You know the name Hershey. It says it right on the bar. Milton Hershey grew up in Derry Church, Pennsylvania, and started a caramel company there. In 1900, he decided to switch to milk chocolate, which was very expensive at the time. He tried lots of different formulas until he hit on the one that became the Hershey bar, the first chocolate bar in the United States.

Milton Hershey didn't just make chocolate. He created a community for the employees who worked in his factory, with schools, parks, churches, housing, an amusement park, and a trolley system. I guess that's why Derry Church, Pennsylvania, changed its name in 1906. Today it's called Hershey, Pennsylvania.

Sylvester Graham (1794–1851)

 It would be cool to have a town named after you. But if you ask me, it would be even cooler to have a *cracker* named after you.

Sylvester Graham was a minister in Connecticut. He believed that living a healthy lifestyle was important. That meant eating a mostly vegetarian diet with no coffee, tea, alcohol, and very little meat.

He also believed that bread should be made with whole grains. So in 1820, he created a healthy snack, which of course came to be called the graham cracker.

John Kellogg (1852–1943) and
Will Kellogg (1860–1951)

 Like Sylvester Graham, Dr. John Kellogg was a big fan of healthy eating. At the health sanitarium he ran with his brother, patients complained that the food was boring. So the Kellogg boys started experimenting to jazz up the

meals. As you read in the last chapter, they invented wheat flakes and corn flakes. Today, of course, you can buy Kellogg's Froot Loops, Apple Jacks, Rice Krispies, Cocoa Krispies, Pringles, Pop-Tarts, and Cheez-Its. The list goes on and on.

By the way, one of the patients at the Kellogg's sanitarium was Charles William Post, who started a cereal company of his own—Post!

Ermal "Ernie" Fraze (1913–1989)

 Ernie Fraze was at a picnic in Dayton, Ohio, in 1959 when he realized he forgot to bring a can opener. He had to take cans over to his car and jam them against the bumper to poke a hole in the tops.

There had to be a better way. So Ernie, who was a machine tool operator, invented the soda can pull-tab. Instead of using a can opener, you just yanked off a little piece of the can to open it.

That caused another problem—those little metal pull-tabs were sharp and dangerous to people and animals. So in 1977, Ernie improved the design so that the little tab pushed *into* the can and stayed attached to it after poking a hole in the metal. That's what we use today.

Oscar Weber Bilby (1870–?)

 One of the burning myster-ies of history is: Who invented the hamburger bun? Well, it *is* a question, anyway.

A few people claim to have invented the hamburger bun, but most researchers give the credit to Oscar Bilby of Tulsa, Oklahoma, in 1891. Before then, hamburgers were served on slices of toast, and they were called patty melts. But Oscar and his wife, Fanny, threw a Fourth of July barbecue, and Fanny baked up a batch of sourdough buns. Oscar decided to put the patties on the buns instead of on toast, and the rest is hamburger history.*

Johnny Appleseed (1774–1845)

 Remember when we went to the school library and Mrs. Roopy was wearing overalls and a pot on her head? That was weird. She was dressed up as Johnny Appleseed. His real name was John Chapman, and he was born in Massachusetts. Chapman lived a simple life, growing apple trees and traveling around the country planting trees and giving apple seeds to the pioneers. He became an American folk hero.

---

*How come Fanny didn't get the credit? She's the one who baked the buns.

Real People or Fake People?

 Many food companies are represented on their packages by the smiling face of a man or woman. Some of them were real people. Others were fictional characters. Arlo and I went undercover to find out who was real and who was fake.

Betty Crocker

 FAKE!

In 1921, the company that made Gold Medal Flour held a puzzle contest. Thirty thousand people sent in entries. Many of them also included letters with questions about baking. The company decided they needed a spokesperson who could answer customers' kitchen questions. Instead of hiring a real person, the advertising agency dreamed up a fictional woman named Betty Crocker.

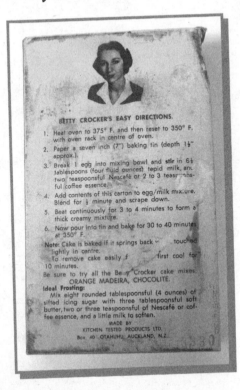

BETTY CROCKER'S EASY DIRECTIONS.

1. Heat oven to 375° F. and then reset to 350° F. with oven rack in centre of oven.
2. Paper a seven inch (7") baking tin (depth 1½" approx.).
3. Break 1 egg into mixing bowl and stir in 6½ tablespoons (four fluid ounces) tepid milk, and two teaspoonsful Nescafé or 2 to 3 teaspoonsful coffee essence.
4. Add contents of this carton to egg/milk mixture. Blend for ½ minute and scrape down.
5. Beat continuously for 3 to 4 minutes to form a thick creamy mixture.
6. Now pour into tin and bake for 30 to 40 minutes at 350° F.

Note: Cake is baked if it springs back when touched lightly in centre.
To remove cake easily first cool for 10 minutes.
Be sure to try all the Betty Crocker cake mixes.
ORANGE MADEIRA, CHOCOLITE.

Ideal Frosting:
Mix eight rounded tablespoonsful (4 ounces) of sifted icing sugar with three tablespoonsful soft butter, two or three teaspoonsful of Nescafé or coffee essence, and a little milk to soften.
MADE BY
KITCHEN TESTED PRODUCTS LTD.
Box 40 OTAHUHU, AUCKLAND, N.Z.

They chose "Betty" because it sounded cheerful and wholesome. "Crocker" was a director of the company that made Gold Medal Flour.

Sara Lee

 REAL!

Charlie Lubin needed a good name for his cheesecakes, so he decided to name them after his eight-year-old daughter, Sara Lee. She actually appeared in some TV commercials over the years. She said her dad told her the product had to be perfect "because he was naming it after me."

Oscar Mayer

 REAL!

Oscar Mayer left Germany to come to America in 1873. He worked at butcher shops in the Chicago area, where many Germans had settled. With the help of his brothers Max and Gottfried, Oscar opened his own shop. Gottfried supplied the recipes for sausages they sold. They were so popular that people lined up to purchase them every day.

Why didn't they name the company Gottfried Mayer? I guess "Oscar Mayer" sounds better than "Gottfried Mayer."

Ben and Jerry

 REAL!

Ben Cohen and Jerry Greenfield were two kids from Brooklyn, New York, who became friends in junior high school. After college, they paid five dollars to take a correspondence course in ice-cream making at Penn State University.

In 1978, they used their savings to open up "Ben & Jerry's Scoop Shop" in an old, renovated Burlington, Vermont, gas station. It was a big success, and now they have scoop shops everywhere from Australia to Turkey. No trip to Vermont is complete without a visit to the Ben & Jerry's factory.

Chef Boyardee

REAL!

Ettore "Hector" Boiardi was born in Italy and came to America in 1914. He was a chef who worked at many restaurants. In

1924, he opened his own place in Cleveland, and his spaghetti was so popular that customers wanted to make it at home. So Boiardi and his brothers started the Chef Boiardi Food Company. The only problem was that Americans had trouble pronouncing "Boiardi," so they changed the spelling to Boyardee.

Jimmy Dean

 REAL!

Jimmy Dean was a popular country music singer and actor from Texas. He even had his own TV show. One day, Jimmy and his brother Don were at a Texas diner when Don ate a tough piece

 of sausage. They wished they could have some with better quality. So they started the Jimmy Dean Sausage Company in 1969. It

quickly became the largest supplier of sausage in America.

Duncan Hines

 REAL!

Duncan Hines was a salesman from Kentucky who was on the road a lot. He kept a notebook in which he listed all his favorite restaurants. He even published a restaurant guide called *Adventures in Good Eating* in 1935. Restaurants displayed the "Duncan Hines Seal of Approval" in their windows. In the 1940s, Hines was approached with the idea of licensing his name for food products. The most popular was a line of cake mixes, and they are still very popular today.

Famous Amos

 REAL!

Wally Amos was a talent agent who represented famous singers, including Simon & Garfunkel, the Temptations, Marvin Gaye, and Diana Ross. But he got tired of show business, and in 1975, he decided to do something completely different—sell cookies!

Amos remembered the wonderful

cookies his aunt Delia used to bake when he was growing up in New York. He started the Famous Amos Chocolate Chip Cookie Company, and it was a huge success. Wally Amos's smiling face was on every bag and box.

Chapter 6

Fast-Food Fast Facts

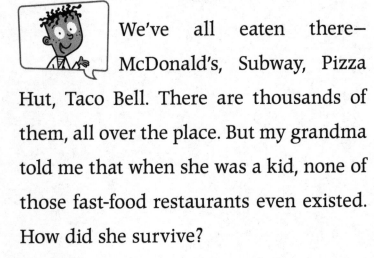

We've all eaten there— McDonald's, Subway, Pizza Hut, Taco Bell. There are thousands of them, all over the place. But my grandma told me that when she was a kid, none of those fast-food restaurants even existed. How did she survive?

I looked up "What was the first fast-food restaurant?" on

my smartphone, and it said it was White Castle. The first one opened in 1921. But my vote goes to . . .

Nathan's Famous

 In 1912, Nathan Handwerker left Poland to start a new life in Brooklyn, New York. He got a job working at a restaurant called Feltman's German Gardens in Coney Island. They sold a lot of hot dogs, but Nathan thought he could make a better one. So he and his wife, Ida, borrowed three hundred dollars and set up a stand on the boardwalk, selling hot dogs for five cents—half the price of Feltman's. They seasoned the dogs with a secret blend of spices handed down from Ida's grandmother.

By 1920, Nathan's Famous was selling 75,000 hot dogs each weekend. But rumors went around that Nathan's half-price hot dogs were no good. People said he used meat that wasn't beef.

So Nathan got the greatest idea in the history of the world. He hired a bunch of guys and dressed them in white lab coats so people would think they were doctors. The "doctors" ate Nathan's hot dogs right in front of the stand, and the public decided that the food was safe to eat.

Here's a fast history of some of our other favorite fast-food chains. . . .

KFC

 During the 1930s, Harland Sanders owned a gas station in Kentucky. In his spare time, he made fried chicken, and he'd sell it to travelers who stopped for gas. The chicken became so popular that the governor named Sanders a Kentucky colonel.

Colonel Sanders started traveling across the country, cooking up chicken in restaurants. He earned a nickel for every chicken that was sold. His company became Kentucky Fried Chicken, and now it's KFC.

In 1956, Colonel Sanders met an ambitious young guy named Dave Thomas. Sanders hired Thomas to turn around four struggling KFC restaurants. They became so successful that Dave Thomas decided to start his own restaurant, and he named it after his daughter Wendy. Today, there are more than six thousand Wendy's restaurants.*

McDonald's

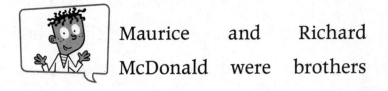 Maurice and Richard McDonald were brothers

---

*On a completely different subject, meatballs are balls of meat, so they have the perfect name.

who owned a hamburger joint in San Bernardino, California. In 1954, an appliance salesman named Ray Kroc noticed that the brothers had ordered eight milkshake machines. He was impressed that such a small shop could sell so many milkshakes, so he went to have a look.

What he found was a simple, efficient restaurant that sold a huge amount of hamburgers at half the price (fifteen cents!) of other restaurants. Customers ordered at the counter, so there was no need for waiters. They didn't need dishwashers, because they used plastic silverware and paper plates. The food arrived quickly because it was cooked ahead of time and warmed under heat lamps.

Kroc knew a great idea when he saw one. He went into business with the McDonald brothers, opening up McDonald's restaurants all over the country.

 The story has a sad ending. Six years later, Kroc bought out the brothers and took over McDonald's. In the agreement, Maurice and Richard weren't even allowed to use their own name anymore. They renamed their restaurant "Big M." Ray Kroc's response—he opened a McDonald's around the block and drove Maurice and Richard out of business.

This McDonald's in Downey, California, is nearly unchanged from when it opened in 1953.

Taco Bell

 Maybe there's something about San Bernardino, California. Taco Bell started there too! And do you know why it's called Taco Bell? Because the guy who started it was Glen Bell.

He was running a burger stand called Bell's Hamburgers and Hot Dogs in 1950. Across the street was a Mexican restaurant. Bell was friendly with the owner, who showed him how to make tacos. Bell opened up his own place called Taco Tia. It was a success, so he kept opening up more and more of them. In 1962, he changed the name to Taco Bell, and now there are seven thousand Taco Bells from China to Panama.

Pizza Hut and Domino's

Nowadays, it seems like there's a pizza place on every corner. But that wasn't the case in 1958. So college students Dan and Frank Carney borrowed six hundred dollars from their mother and bought used equipment to start the first Pizza Hut in Wichita, Kansas. Now there are over thirteen thousand.

Domino's was also started by two brothers, Tom and Jim Monaghan, in Ypsilanti, Michigan. Within a year, Jim traded his share of the business for the old Volkswagen Beetle the brothers were using to make deliveries.

Speaking of deliveries, on his first delivery, Tom Monaghan met his future wife, Marjorie. They've been married for over fifty years.

Dunkin' Donuts and Krispy Kreme

 During World War II, Bill Rosenberg worked at Quincy Shipyards in Massachusetts. There weren't many places to go for lunch, so he bought some trucks and began to sell sandwiches, coffee, doughnuts, and snacks from them. When he saw that half his sales came from coffee and doughnuts, Bill decided to open a little place that just sold coffee for ten cents and doughnuts for a nickel.

It took off, but he didn't like the name—Open Kettle. He noticed that customers liked to dunk their doughnuts in the coffee, so he changed the name to Dunkin' Donuts.

 Krispy Kreme was started by Vernon Rudolph in the 1930s. He bought a secret recipe from a chef in New Orleans and started making doughnuts in Winston-Salem, North Carolina. Rudolph was selling his doughnuts to local grocery stores, but the smell of them baking was so powerful that people walking by asked how they could get them. So Rudolph cut a hole in the wall of the building and started selling hot doughnuts directly to customers. And that's the hole story.

Subway

 In 1965, Fred DeLuca was a seventeen-year-old kid in Brooklyn, New York. He wanted to go to college to become a doctor, but he didn't have enough money. At a barbecue, Fred asked a family friend, Peter Buck, for a college loan. Buck wouldn't give it to him. Instead, he suggested that Fred open up a sandwich shop, and invested a thousand dollars to get it started.

Together, they opened Pete's Super Submarine in Bridgeport, Connecticut. Later they changed the name to Pete's Subway, and finally Subway in 1968.

Today, there are more Subway locations—over 44,000—than any other fast-food chain.

Fred DeLuca never did become a doctor. But he stayed in school while Subway was growing, and in 1971 he graduated from the University of Bridgeport.

Dairy Queen and Baskin-Robbins

Sherb's was the name of three ice-cream parlors in Kankakee, Illinois. They were owned by Sherb Noble. One day in 1938, his suppliers, Bradley and Jack "Grandpa" McCullough, told Sherb they had invented a new kind of ice cream—soft ice cream.

Sherb agreed to try the stuff at one of his stores, and held an "all-you-can-eat-for-ten-cents" sale. Two hours later, sixteen hundred servings had been sold. The store was so mobbed with customers that Sherb was afraid they were going to break the front window. That led to the first Dairy Queen in Joliet, Illinois.

 Around the same time, Irv Robbins was working in his father's ice-cream shop in Tacoma,

Washington. Irv was bored with chocolate and vanilla, so he started to experiment with other flavors. A few years later, Irv's brother-in-law Burt Baskin opened an ice-cream shop in Pasadena, California. Baskin and Robbins decided to combine forces. They flipped a coin to decide whose name would go first on the sign. As you can guess, Baskin won.

Baskin-Robbins has had more than a thousand flavors, plus some that were tested but never made—ketchup, grape Britain, and lox and bagels.

 Fun fast fact: Barack and Michelle Obama had their

first kiss at a Baskin-Robbins in Chicago.
Isn't that romantic, Arlo?

 Yuck! Gross!

Chapter 7

What Is It?

We eat all kinds of stuff every day, and sometimes we have no idea what we're putting in our mouth. Isn't that weird? Well, here are some fast facts on foods you may be wondering about. . . .

Yogurt

What is it, anyway? When

fresh milk is left in a container with friendly bacteria, it thickens. The word "yogurt" comes from Turkey. Arlo, do you know the difference between Greek yogurt and other yogurt?

 Greek yogurt has more grease in it?

 There's no grease in yogurt! Greek yogurt is thicker and creamier because the whey is removed.

 No whey!

 Whey is the watery part of

milk. Taking it out makes the yogurt denser. Also, Greek yogurt has more protein and less sugar.

Jell-O

 Arlo, do you like eating cow and pig bones?

 Yum! They're my favorite foods!

 Then you probably like Jell-O, because that's what it's made from.

 WHAT?!

The gelatin in Jell-O is what makes it jiggly. Gelatin is a processed version of a protein called collagen that's in many animals. So the animal parts are ground up, treated with acid to release the collagen, and then boiled to form gelatin. The gelatin is dried and ground into a fine powder. Jell-O also has water, sugar or artificial sweetener, artificial flavor, and food coloring in it.

Food Coloring

 Speaking of which, there used to be clear Pepsi, pink margarine, and green ketchup. Gross, right? Certain colors seem to go well with certain flavors. Oranges are orange. If you ask me, an orange drink should look like an orange. Red drinks should taste like berries. Purple lollipops should taste like grapes. Nobody wants to eat a gray hot dog or a red banana.

 Because of this, companies dye their packaged food so it looks more appetizing. So if your Cheez

Doodles look particularly orange and your mint chip ice cream looks particularly green, you know why.

 There's another way to color food. The Deli Garage, a German company, makes edible spray paint! It's called Food Finish, and you can spray it on any food. It comes in red, blue, gold, and silver.

That's weird.

Butter and Margarine

 Butter is made by churning milk or cream. This separates

the butterfat (solids) from the buttermilk (liquids). Margarine doesn't have any milk in it. It's made from vegetable oil, water, salt, and emulsifiers, which are additives that help liquids mix. Margarine has to have a minimum fat content of 80 percent. If it's less than that, it's called a spread.

SPAM

 SPAM is made from cooked pork, salt, water, potato starch (to keep the meat moist), sugar, and sodium nitrate (a preservative). It was introduced in 1937 and became popular

during World War II, because soldiers could eat it right out of the can. In 1941, a hundred million pounds of SPAM were sent overseas to feed Allied troops.

There's something about SPAM that is funny. Here are some fun SPAM facts . . .

—There's a museum devoted to SPAM in Austin, Minnesota. It's called the SPAM Museum, so it has the perfect name.

—A "canjo" is a banjo made out of a SPAM can.

—After World War II, the Hormel Company (which makes SPAM) hired an all-female military-style band to promote their products. They were called the Spamettes.

—If you wanted to circle the earth with SPAM (and who wouldn't?), you would need 415,469,599 cans.

—The comedy group Monty Python made a hilarious skit about SPAM.

Cheese

 Cheese is made from four things: milk, salt, a "good bacteria," and rennet. Rennet is an enzyme that makes milk separate into a solid and a liquid. Cheese makers can adjust that basic recipe to make hundreds of kinds of cheeses. Plus, they can make it with the milk of cows, goats, sheep, buffalo, reindeer, camels, and even yaks. Yak cheese!

 So what's Velveeta? I like that stuff. It says "cheese product" on the box.

Velveeta is a kind of processed cheese. That's cheese made from cheeses that are remelted, and then milk, cream, or butter is added to it. Sometimes coloring, sweeteners, seasonings, and preservatives are added too. American cheese is also processed cheese. The Food and Drug Administration doesn't consider it "real" cheese, so it has to be labeled "cheese product" or "cheese food."

Whipped Cream

 Whipped cream is cream that's whipped (so it has the perfect name) until it's light and fluffy. Sugar is usually added to make it sweeter. It's yummy, especially on ice cream!

So what's Cool Whip?

Cool Whip and Reddi-Wip are whipped cream substitutes. They have cream in them, but they also have water, vegetable oil, corn syrup, skimmed milk, and chemical additives.

Reddi-Wip comes in a can with an aerosol nozzle. Nitrous oxide inside the can mixes with the other ingredients and whips it all up as it shoots out of the nozzle. Aaron "Bunny" Lapin invented the nozzle in 1955, and he was called the Whipped Cream King.

Sausage and Hot Dogs

 Centuries ago, people hunted animals for food. They didn't want to waste anything, so when they killed an animal, they tried to use every part of it. That's how the sausage was born.

A sausage is made from ground meat (usually pork, beef, or veal) mixed with salt and seasonings. Then they stuff this stuff into a skin called a casing, which is made from the small intestines of cows, hogs, or sheep. Are you grossed out yet? Keep reading.

A hot dog is a type of sausage. They're called frankfurters because they were originally made in Frankfurt, Germany.* German immigrants brought them to America in the late 1800s.

What's inside a hot dog? All kinds of stuff. They start with beef or pork trimmings. Those are the lower-grade parts of an animal—muscle parts, fatty tissue, feet, skin, blood, liver, head meat. Are you grossed out yet?

All that stuff is cooked and ground

---

*People in Frankfurt are called Frankfurters, and people from Hamburg are called Hamburgers. That must be weird.

up. Then they add salt, spices, water, and sometimes corn syrup or fillers like bread crumbs or flour. After that, all that stuff is pumped into casings.

So, are you grossed out *now*?

Chapter 8

More Weird Food Facts

 In France, from 1748 to 1772, it was illegal to grow potatoes.

 The first supermarket was a Piggly Wiggly opened by Clarence Saunders in 1916 in Memphis, Tennessee. Why did he call it Piggly Wiggly? The story is told that somebody asked

Saunders why he chose such a weird name, and he replied, "So people will ask that very question."

A Piggly Wiggly in Chicago, 1926

 "Masticate" means "to chew." Horace Fletcher (1849–1919) was a health food expert who was known as "The Great Masticator." He claimed

that people should chew their food a hundred times a minute before swallowing it. I wouldn't want to eat dinner with that guy!

 Which US city eats the most hot dogs? Los Angeles! Over

95 million hot dogs were eaten there in 2012.

PB&J

 Many people think George Washington Carver invented peanut butter. Actually, the Aztecs were mashing peanuts into a paste thousands of years ago.

 At least four people get credit for inventing modern peanut butter and the machines that make it. Marcellus Gilmore Edson of Canada patented a kind of peanut paste in 1884. In 1895, Dr. John Harvey Kellogg (of

Kellogg's cereal) sold peanut butter as a healthy food for people who didn't have teeth. In 1903, Dr. Ambrose Straub of St. Louis patented a machine that made peanut butter. And in 1922, a chemist named Joseph Rosefield invented the process for making *smooth* peanut butter. He sold his invention to the company that created Peter Pan peanut butter, and later he returned to the peanut butter biz by introducing Skippy.

Jelly is another story. Before there were refrigerators (around 1913), you couldn't get fruits that were out of season. So people started canning jams, *jellies*, and preserves so there would be fruit all year round.

I know what you're thinking. Who was the genius who came up with the greatest invention in the history of the world—the peanut butter and jelly sandwich?

 Well, nobody knows for sure who was the first person to spread peanut butter and jelly on bread. We *do* know the first person to write about it. It was Julia Davis Chandler, who put a recipe for my favorite food in the 1901 *Boston Cooking-School Magazine*. So she gets credit.

 I'm going to go with Bob PB&J.

Did you know that January is National Oatmeal Month, and February is Return Shopping Carts to the Supermarket Month? It's true! We don't make this stuff up. Look it up in July. That's National Pickle Month.

 In 1915, you could buy lunch for fifteen cents. *Fifteen cents!* Of course, everything was cheaper a century ago. You could buy a loaf of bread for seven cents, a quart of milk for nine cents, or a dozen eggs for thirty-four cents.

 In Scotland, they call toffee

"tablet." It's so hard that you can't break it with your teeth. So they sell it with a little hammer.

 If you like licorice, buy black Twizzlers. Red Twizzlers don't have any licorice in them. They're made out of corn syrup, wheat flour, and artificial flavoring.

You've heard of state flags, state birds, and state flowers. Well, Massachusetts and Pennsylvania named the chocolate chip cookie as their "state cookie."

Super Sunday

 The Super Bowl is famous for two things—football and eating. Domino's sells about twelve million slices of pizza on Super Bowl Sunday. Americans will eat 139 million pounds of avocados, mostly in the form of guacamole. And if you're going to eat guacamole, you're going to need tortilla chips—8.2 million pounds of it.

According to the National Chicken Council (yes, that's a thing), 1.35 *billion* chicken wings are eaten on Super Bowl Sunday. That's a lot of wings! I wonder what they do with the rest of the chicken.

It seems like such a waste to just eat the wings.

 When Admiral Richard Byrd explored Antarctica in 1928, he brought along two and a half tons of Necco Wafers.

 Museums are boring. Who wants to look at a bunch of

paintings on a wall? But there's one museum I like to visit. It's the Candy Wrapper Museum. Yes, it's a museum filled with candy wrappers, so it has the perfect name. And the best part is, it's online so you can visit it no matter where you live.

 The rock group Van Halen is famous for songs like "Jump" and "Panama." Van Halen was also famous for insisting their dressing room have a bowl of M&M's in it, and that all the brown M&M's had to be removed.

The Good Old Days?

Many of us have it easy these days. We go to the supermarket and buy a week's worth of food. But back in colonial times, there were no supermarkets. There were no convenience foods or fast-food restaurants. People ate what they could grow, raise, fish, or hunt. So they ate stuff like beaver tail, squirrel, eel, turtle soup, and bread made from acorns. One popular dish was clabber, which was raw milk that was left to go sour so it could thicken before being eaten.

Gross! They even ate moose nose! That's right. Nothing got wasted. The nose of the moose was boiled and cut into thin slices or mashed into a paste.

They didn't have refrigerators in those days either. They preserved food by salting, smoking, pickling, and making jam or marmalade.

 Food was often scarce during the Civil War, especially in the South. Soldiers survived on a lot of canned beans and salt pork.

 During the Great Depression in the 1930s, lots of people lost their jobs and couldn't afford food. They were lucky if there was a soup kitchen where they could get a free meal.

There are many poor people who are

hungry today too, all over the world. So we shouldn't take for granted the food we can get so easily.

 In Finland, people eat tar. They have tar-flavored ice cream and tar-flavored licorice candy called *tervaleijona*.*

Do you know who invented energy bars, portable yogurt, instant coffee, and all the other grab-and-go snacks we eat? The US military! It has been said that an army travels on its

_____

*I just thought I'd mention that "tar" is "rat" spelled backward.

stomach, and soldiers in the field can't stop off at the nearest restaurant when their stomachs start to growl. So the military created portable packaged foods that soldiers could eat on the go. It turned out that other people liked them too— working parents, hikers, dieters, office workers, and kids who needed a quick snack.

Weird Food World Records

 Remember the time Mr. Tony (who is full of baloney) helped us make the biggest pizza in the world? He used a flamethrower to heat it up.

Well, here are some other weird food records . . .

In 2018, Joey Chestnut ate seventy-four hot dogs in ten minutes. It was at Nathan's Famous Fourth of July Hot Dog Eating Contest in Coney Island. In 2017,

Ashrita Furman from New York balanced 123 scoops of ice cream on one cone. He also holds the record for the most *Guinness World Records* titles.

 In 2011, Ross McCurdy from Kingston, Washington, cracked thirty-two eggs with one hand in one minute.

 In 1999, Gary Bashaw Jr. from Los Angeles swallowed a bunch of milkshake ingredients. Then he shot 1.82 ounces of milkshake out of his nose. That gave him the Guinness World Record for "Most Milkshake Dispensed Through the Nose."

 In 2012, 3,463 people at the University of Illinois set the record for "Most People Husking Corn at One Time."

 In 2000, Rob Williams made a bologna sandwich in less than two minutes. That may not seem very impressive, except for the fact that he only used his feet.

 When it comes to weird food records, nobody is weirder than the British. Here are a few records set by British people . . .

Freddie Yauner designed a toaster that can launch a piece of bread more than

eight feet in the air. It's called the Moaster.

In 2012, 890 people in Sheffield flipped pancakes all at the same time. Forty of them dropped their pancake and were disqualified.

In 2005, Colin Shirlow ate 233 oysters in three minutes.

In 2017, Lewis Bacon set a record for running a half marathon. He was dressed as a hot dog. And his name is Bacon.

Well, it looks like we've run out of pages, Arlo.

 No! I have one last fast fact! At the Modern Toilet Restaurant in Taipei, each customer sits on a toilet and eats their meal at a sink or bath-tub with a glass top. Not only that, but the food is served in a bowl shaped like a toilet. So you can sit on the toilet and eat out of a toilet at the same time!

Ice cream from the Modern Toilet restaurant

Arlo!

The Ending

 Congrats, weirdos! Now you know *everything* there is to know about food.

 They do *not*, Arlo.

 Well, that's true. I barely said

anything about how food turns into pee and poop after you eat it. Would you like to hear more about that?

 No! But there's lots more cool stuff to know about food. You can learn just by reading the labels on the foods you eat.

 Reading? Learning? Ugh, disgusting!

 Oh, Arlo. You *know* that learning new stuff is cool. Isn't it fun to impress grown-ups with how smart you are? They think kids are a

bunch of dumbheads who don't know anything. But we'll show *them*!

 That's right! You think the stuff in this book was weird? We didn't have room to talk about all the weird stuff people eat that isn't even food. Go ahead. Look this stuff up.

Yes. Maybe you'll be able to convince your parents that magician Todd Robbins has eaten over five thousand lightbulbs. Maybe you'll be able to convince your teacher that Leon Samson, the Australian circus strongman, won a bet by eating a whole car (it took four years). Maybe you'll be able to convince your librarian that Michel Lotito from France ate eighteen bicycles, fifteen shopping carts, seven televisions, two beds, a pair of skis, and an *airplane*.

 But it won't be easy!

I Like WEIRD Books.

My Weird School

Discover more in the My Weird School series from Dan Gutman

My Weirder School

My Weirdest School

My Weirder-est School

My Weird School Fast Facts

My Weird School Daze

My Weird Tips